Better Homes and Gardens®

style

on a budget

Better Homes and Gardens® Books
Des Moines, Iowa

Better Homes and Gardens® Books
An imprint of Meredith® Books

Style on a Budget
Editor: Vicki L. Ingham
Contributing Editor: Rebecca Jerdee
Design: The Design Office of Jerry J. Rank
Copy Chief: Terri Fredrickson
Copy and Production Editor: Victoria Forlini
Editorial Operations Manager: Karen Schirm
Managers, Book Production: Pam Kvitne, Marjorie J. Schenkelberg
Contributing Copy Editor: Jane Woychick
Contributing Proofreaders: Nancy Ruhling, Sue Fetters, Judy Friedman
Indexer: Sharon Duffy
Electronic Production Coordinator: Paula Forest
Editorial and Design Assistants: Kaye Chabot, Karen McFadden, Mary Lee Gavin

Meredith® Books
Publisher and Editor in Chief: James D. Blume
Design Director: Matt Strelecki
Managing Editor: Gregory H. Kayko
Executive Editor, Home Decorating and Design: Denise L. Caringer

Director, Operations: George A. Susral
Director, Production: Douglas M. Johnston

Vice President, General Manager: Douglas J. Guendel

***Better Homes and Gardens*® Magazine**
Editor in Chief: Karol DeWulf Nickell

Meredith Publishing Group
President, Publishing Group: Stephen M. Lacy
Vice President-Publishing Director: Bob Mate

Meredith Corporation
Chairman and Chief Executive Officer: William T. Kerr

Chairman of the Executive Committee: E. T. Meredith III

All of us at Better Homes and Gardens® Books are dedicated to providing you with information and ideas to enhance your home. We welcome your comments and suggestions. Write to us at: Better Homes and Gardens Books, Home Decorating and Design Editorial Department, 1716 Locust St., Des Moines, IA 50309-3023.

If you would like to purchase any of our home decorating and design, cooking, crafts, gardening, or home improvement books, check wherever quality books are sold. Or visit us at: bhgbooks.com

contents

getting
started

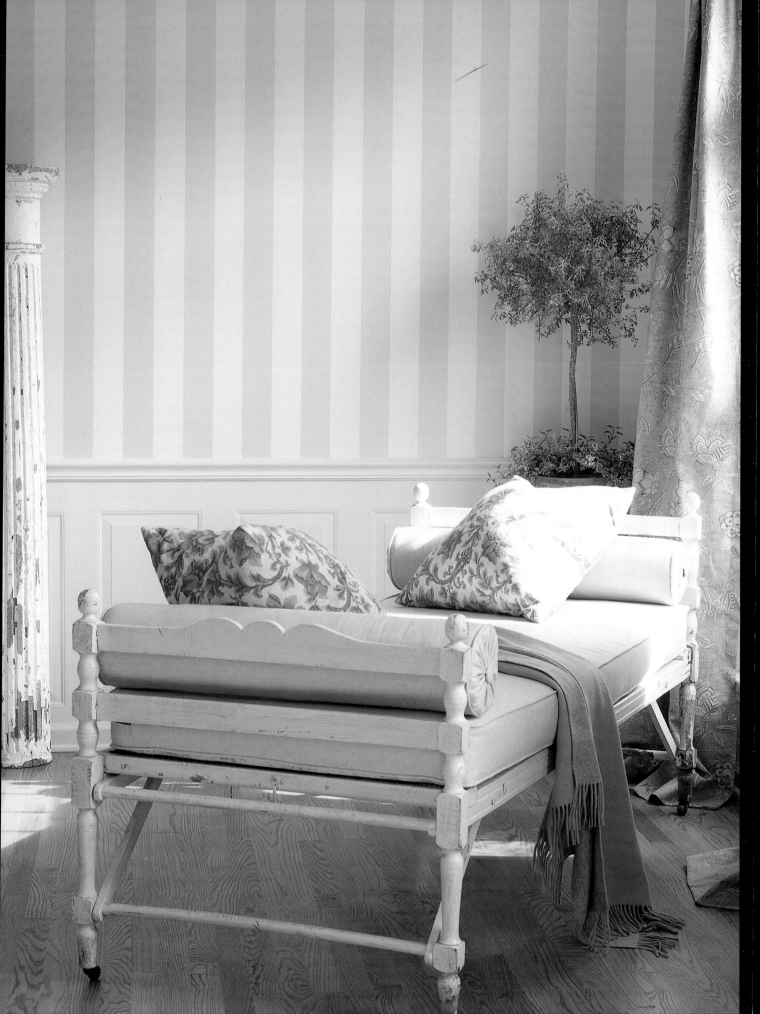

acquaint yourself with the elements of **good design** by exposing yourself to as many design **influences** as possible: museums, art galleries, fine furniture stores, **books**, and magazines. You may not be able to afford the **very best**, but you'll be able to **recognize well-designed** furnishings when you see them.

good proportions, pleasing lines, and quality aren't the exclusive domain of high-priced, top-of-the-line furnishings. The real measure of an object's worth lies in how useful or pleasing it is to you and how well it fits in your home. The classic upholstered pieces, *above*, surround a plank coffee table. Knitting baskets provide extra storage.

know your style

plan on paper It doesn't cost anything to plan your evolving decorating style and fully furnished home or to make better use of what you already have. Space is a coveted commodity, so explore options for each room on graph paper. Arrange your own cut-to-scale templates, *left,* or use the arranging kit that begins on page 137. Pencil in architectural, fixed features first. Then site in major furniture pieces, allowing for traffic zones: 3 feet for interior doors, 4 feet for entries, and at least 30 inches for walkways. For conversation areas, group sofas and chairs a maximum of 8 feet apart. Leave 14 to 18 inches between a sofa and coffee table and at least 3 feet of pull-out space behind dining chairs. **dream your rooms** before they happen. Dreams are free for the imagining, and they prepare you for spotting the perfect furniture piece when it crosses your path. **make a wish list** of furnishings you'd like to own. Add the approximate costs or the prices you are willing to pay for those pieces. Apply a realistic budget to the list to establish a purchasing time frame and project how much money you'll need to set aside to carry out your plan.

the pared-down look is an elegant approach to interior design. It has an unexpected benefit:
Less furniture costs less money. A limited number of furniture pieces creates an eye-catching study in
simplicity. Undecorated windows make a fitting backdrop for such a clean arrangement of furnishings.

keep it simple

shop import stores for unusual, artful pieces with good lines, *above*. Affordable prices are the hallmark of import stores, and the style of imported handmade furniture pieces is usually excellent. **start with one great piece** to set the scene. A signature bed is the starting point for the master bedroom, *left*. Once your "great piece" is in place, use budget-conscious extras to fill out the rest of the room. For example, cover a decorator table with a simple white tablecloth, add a family heirloom, and soften bare spots with dried flowers. **buy the best** you can afford. You'll be better off (and so will your bank account). This may mean buying one good-quality piece, such as a sofa, and making do with inexpensive interim pieces until you're able to afford the other furnishings you want. The chaise, *opposite,* occupies an elegantly simple room. A secondhand side table does butler duty, and discount-store sheers provide privacy and sun control. The chaise is a star-quality piece of furniture that always will be a great investment.

build a wardrobe of mix-and-match furnishings

explore specialty shops, discount warehouses, and mail-order outlets for good-quality furnishings at reasonable prices. Terrific bargains also can be found at auctions, flea markets, secondhand shops, and garage sales. Don't buy something only because the price is right, however; as the old saying goes, "You get what you pay for." A classic, good quality sofa, *above*, is the backbone in a room full of specialty pieces.

shop smart Make "browse first, buy later" your furniture shopping credo. It doesn't pay to be impulsive with high-ticket items. Peruse books and magazines to learn about style and construction; then compare items in all price ranges. A mix-don't-match philosophy and snappy neutral colors, *opposite,* weave together diverse pieces. **judge quality** Sit on it, lean on it, lift it up, and turn it over to check construction. Upholstery frames, *below,* should be kiln-dried, seasoned hardwood joined by dowels or interlocking pieces (not butted together). Tempered-steel springs are coil or sagless; eight-way hand-tied coils denote good quality. Polyurethane foam is the most common filling; down, which is softer, is more expensive. **know your woods** When shopping for case goods, check hangtags and labels to learn which woods and veneers are used in different pieces. Look for strong construction where pieces bear the most weight—legs, shelves, braces, and drawers. Doors and drawers should open and shut easily, and finishes should be hard and smooth with no visible imperfections.

be patient Buy one piece at a time, savoring the purchase. If you buy antiques, wood frames should be sound with no signs of termites or dry rot. If legs are wobbly, finishes are marred, or upholstery is worn, factor repairs into the total cost before you decide to buy. A piece is more valuable if it has a known maker and date, fine design, original hardware and finish, and no damage or repairs. Your patient, one-at-a-time purchases will pay off in a distinctive decorating style developed over years.

let your decorating style
evolve

paint and save

paint

in a can is like a genie in a bottle: **It transforms whatever it touches.** Beyond that, it's **liquid gold,** money in the decorating bank. For just a few dollars and a little time, paint rewards you with **big decorative returns.** Turn these pages for paint ideas to **revitalize and refresh** your rooms.

pale and airy The lightest tints of yellow warm the architecturally interesting walls of this dining room without creating jarring contrasts. More intense colors could busy the room or compete with the furniture. With only hints of pale color, the yellows stay quietly in the background, allowing the antique chairs and painted pedestal table to be the focal points of the room.

paint gives you the
power to
express a mood

neutral & serene Grant your wish for a quiet, calm, yet strong space by painting with taupes, browns, grays, and whites. A chair rail like the one shown, *far left,* suggests painting with two colors. For drama, use light and dark neutrals; for a soft, subtle look, choose two shades of the same color. Visually anchor the space by painting the darker shade below the chair rail and the lighter one on top. **cool & restful** Blues and greens are associated with peace and serenity. Light versions (tints) open rooms, keeping the mood airy and fresh. Dark blues and greens (shades) give rooms weight, drama, and depth; grayed blues and greens work like neutrals. Painting the ceiling a close or matching color completely wraps a room with the mood. **warm & vivacious** Some like it hot. If that's your style, paint rooms with bold reds, pinks, and yellows. Be careful, though: Large expanses of intense or saturated versions of these warm colors can wear you out. To use intense reds or oranges successfully, try painting only one wall as an accent in a room. Or use a brilliant hue on one or two pieces of furniture to give a room a jolt of color.

accent a room's architecture

define a room with paint. Woodwork draws lines around a room. Boring, featureless woodwork is best left quietly painted the same color as the walls, but grand and beautiful woodwork deserves to be a main attraction in a room. Emphasize it with high-gloss paint that contrasts with the wall color. On light walls, *above,* dark woodwork plays a key role in a monochromatic (green) color scheme. To achieve the same effect on dark walls, paint the woodwork light. **unify furnishings** with matching stains and paint. Like it quiet, earthy, and serene? Put it in neutral. The dining room, *right,* combines woodsy stains with paint the color of yellow earth and pottery. A low-contrast color scheme covers every surface: walls, furniture, floor, beams, and woodwork. Color choices were pulled from the wood grain of the elegant, polished tabletop. **accentuate** a beautiful ceiling if you're lucky enough to have one. Ceilings often are ignored, simply painted white to reflect the light coming in through the windows. In a room with plenty of light, however, a colored ceiling could better serve the space, extending the scheme of the room in a continuous and seamless style. In the dining room, *far right,* paint colors on the ceiling echo the hues in the finely striped wallcovering.

create **special**
effects

fair & square Softly mingled colors within a grid, *opposite,* provide a serene backdrop for furniture. A special double roller, *left,* blends a light base-coat color with a darker hue. Keeping the colors pale and only two shades apart on a paint store color card creates a subtle pattern you can use throughout a room. If you use two highly contrasting colors, reserve the bold pattern for an accent wall. Use your wall height to determine the size of your squares, leaving a 3-inch border around each square (these squares are 20¼ inches). Cut the square from cardboard. Draw level lines 3 inches below the ceiling and 3 inches above the floor; then use the cardboard square and ruler to mark the position of the squares along the horizontal. Repeat along the vertical. Use low-tack painter's tape to mask off the borders; apply paint. When the paint is dry, remove the tape. | **THE DOUBLE ROLLER, new on the market, allows you to apply two colors at once. Varying the direction of your strokes produces a third, marbled tone. The roller comes in a kit with patterned roller covers and a double roller tray.**

stripe it rich Paneling, *above,* provides an instant canvas for experimenting with stripes; the lines are drawn in already. If you don't have paneling, use a plumb bob or level to pencil in stripes. Prime and paint the wall the lighter color first. Then mask alternating sections with tape and roll on stripes in the darker color. For a touch of elegance, add a fleur-de-lis stamp randomly where the stripes meet.

do the shimmer Iridescent squares seem to float up the wall like soap bubbles, adding a lot of decorating pop for little effort. Begin by cutting a square in the center of a piece of lightweight poster board (this square is 3 inches; the poster board is 18×24 inches). Use a crafts knife and a metal ruler, and keep the square's edges parallel with those of the poster board. Seal this homemade stencil with polyurethane spray so it's easy to wipe clean. Before painting, tape up paper squares cut slightly smaller than your stencil; play with their positions until you find an arrangement you like. Then spray the back of the stencil with stencil adhesive (available at crafts stores) and stick the stencil to the wall over one of the squares. Check with a level to be sure the stencil is plumb; remove the paper square and spray. Repeat for remaining squares. **TEST A SQUARE OF PAINT (metallic copper is shown) before doing the whole wall. If it tends to rub off, seal it with polyurethane. To do this, reposition the stencil over the dried paint and then spray on the polyurethane sealant.**

over the line

This double-stripe pattern, *below,* is uniform, but doesn't look stiff or highly perfected. That's because the vertical lines are painted freehand, so they dance a little. The paint is a metallic copper artist's acrylic (available in tubes at art stores), so it's more reflective than even a high-gloss wall paint. To prepare the lines, mark alternating 6- and 9-inch intervals along the top and bottom of the wall with a pencil. Use a level and straightedge to lightly draw in vertical guidelines. For the best results, center a stripe over a doorway or window and work out from there. Mix a small amount of paint with a few drops of water, until the mixture has the consistency of heavy cream. Then, using even pressure, apply the paint over the pencil lines. Paint a second strip ¼ inch to the right of the first (if you're left-handed, work from right to left). Draw another guide or simply freehand it. **| USE A SMALL ARTIST'S BRUSH with 1⅛-inch bristles. Start at the top with your strokes, standing under your brush and looking where you are going (don't watch the brush). When the color starts to thin, reload the brush with paint.**

striping a porch floor

Prepare the porch floor by scraping away old flaking paint, filling any gouges, and sanding the surface smooth. Pound in any nails that have risen from the floorboards. Thoroughly clean the floor, including the spaces between boards. Prime the surface with a good-quality primer; then paint with one or two coats of floor paint in a light cream color.

|USE 1-INCH-WIDE LOW-TACK PAINTER'S TAPE to create the striped design, *above*. The floor is made up of alternating 5-inch-wide and 7-inch-wide planks. The full width of the 5-inch-wide boards is painted a dark green. Each 7-inch-wide board is painted with two narrow green stripes, 1 inch in from each edge. (Adjust the pattern to fit the boards of your floor, if necessary.) First, tape off the edges of every 5-inch-wide plank. On the 7-inch boards, run a row of painter's tape parallel to the first set of tapes, leaving $\frac{1}{2}$ inch of floor exposed between the tapes. Run a rigid plastic card along the tapes to seal them to the floor. Paint the 5-inch-wide planks and the narrow stripes green or a color of your choice. Leave the remaining 4-inch-wide spaces between the narrow stripes cream-colored. Remove the tapes shortly after the paint is dry to reveal the pattern.

painting over vinyl

Bathe an old bathroom floor in fresh color and add a whimsical stamped design across the surface. Vinyl that is in good shape but outdated in either pattern or color is a prime candidate for painting. If the floor is worn, cracked, or flaking, however, paint will only emphasize the problem. Flat- or pebble-surfaced floors can handle almost any stamped design. If your vinyl has an embossed pattern, choose a rubber stamp that accommodates both the shape and design of the flooring. Deep-cut stamps work best. **WHEN DECIDING** whether to paint, remember that hard-surface vinyls accept paint better than softer types. To make sure the paint sticks, remove any wax and thoroughly clean the vinyl. Apply a liquid sanding solution to roughen the surface. Prime the surface, then apply one or two coats of latex floor paint. Floor paint withstands traffic, suits many types of floors, and works both indoors and outdoors. For a stamped design, paint a second color onto a stamp and apply the stamp randomly across the floor. Top with two coats of nonyellowing, water-based polyurethane.

windsor bench To age a secondhand or unfinished bench like the one *above,* purchase a primer, black and white acrylic paints, crackle medium (available at crafts stores), and a clear, water-based varnish. Practice the process on a board first. Then sand the bench well, wipe it clean with a tack cloth, and cover it with primer. Let it dry, then sand again. Paint the entire bench black. Let it dry and apply a second coat if necessary. Apply the crackle medium to the seat of the bench, following the manufacturer's instructions. For fine cracks, apply a thin coat; for larger cracks, apply a thicker coat. Let the medium dry until it's tacky to the touch; when you can leave a fingerprint in the medium, it's dry enough.

STARTING AT ONE END of the bench and following the grain of the wood, quickly brush white paint over the seat. Do not rebrush an area after you apply the paint. (Rebrushing will interfere with the crackling.) The direction of your brushstroke determines the direction of the crackling. For long cracks that follow the wood grain, make long straight strokes. To create a web of cracks, apply the top coat of paint with short, slip-slap strokes, brushing in a different direction with each stroke. As the paint dries, cracks will appear. Let the paint dry completely and seal the entire bench with varnish.

"antique" cupboard Give an unfinished cupboard the look and status of a valuable antique with a brand-new finish of ivory over oak. You'll need crackle medium (available in crafts stores) and a paint color to complement the room where the furniture will be. First, practice the finish on a board. Then lightly sand the cupboard; remove dust with a tack cloth and brush on the base coat over raw wood. Allow to dry. Apply the crackle medium, following the manufacturer's directions. Lightly apply the top coat of paint. Do not brush over or attempt to touch up the top coat. Doing so interferes with the crackling. When the furniture piece is crackled and dry, seal the entire surface with polyurethane.

age it with a crackle finish

chairs that rock Put a fresh spin on classic porch rockers with a mix of four pretty pastels. Any porch rocker with slats will do for this project, as long as all the chairs are the same. Work out your color combinations before beginning the project. Sand and prime the chairs. Paint each chair one color and use three other colors for accents. Seal the chairs with an exterior sealer if they will be used outdoors. **garden bench** Prepare an unfinished bench with a primer before painting it with two colors of exterior paint. (Use a tinted primer under yellows, yellow-greens, and oranges. Otherwise, you'll need to apply additional coats of paint for good coverage because these colors contain less pigment than other colors.) After the primer dries, paint the bench with your chosen colors. To blend with the garden, use olive green and a medium green the color of grass. **more ideas** Change the bench colors if your setting is different from the stonework patio shown here. ■ For a seaside environment, choose blue and white paint colors or two shades of aqua or blue-green. ■ Consider painting the bench a single color, such as dark olive green on a traditional porch with traditional dark green rocking chairs.

take color outside

super store stand-ins

decorating

to go is a sign of the 21st century— **designed to save you time and money.** Superstores appeal to the **common sense** part of yourself, the fiscally prudent self that's thrilled by **style at bargain-basement prices.** This chapter is full of rooms that began with discount department store purchases.

easy pieces Decorating superstores give new meaning to carryout:
An SUV or large vehicle will get you home with lightweight wicker pieces,
knockdown shelving, and not-so-serious accessories. After the purchase of a
sofa from a catalog, low-priced home furnishings filled the rest of this room
to give it a stylish, graceful, and happy look.

shopping cart pleasures
have never been so good

off-the-shelf dining Many discount superstores tout low prices, but some also address the important issue of style, seeking to provide the consumer with good-looking yet inexpensive home furnishings. Furniture pieces often come in flat-packs that require some assembly; it's a fast and affordable way to fill a room and make it useable. The dining room, *opposite,* is a winner, thanks to large posters, an area rug, and an unfinished table-and-chairs set. Paint did the rest, giving the room a sparkling presence. **bedroom basics** Sometimes cheap chic equals sophisticated simplicity. Note the simple, nonchalant roller shade window treatment, ready-to-assemble bedside chest, comfy bedding, and ginger-jar lamp in the bedroom, *above.* These superstore purchases provide the starting points for a guest room assembled from hand-me-downs.

more ideas Even sofas and upholstered chairs come in flat-packs. ■ Create a seating group with two superstore chairs and an antique love seat. Set the love seat along a wall and place a barrel chair at each end to make a U-shape conversation area. ■ Set up a home office with flat-pack, some-assembly-required units. Remember to put a desk light in your shopping cart.

unfinished furniture
lets you

cottage style is defined by a white-painted metal headboard; unfinished, natural-stained storage pieces; and a comfortable beige and white color scheme, *left*. Covering one accent wall with striped paper is more affordable than covering all four walls, and using a headboard alone costs less than an entire bed frame. Create **contemporary** style with straight-lined unfinished chests stacked in a traditional chest-on-chest formation, *below*. Remove the feet on the small chest before painting all surfaces with two or three coats of white enamel. Accessorize with all-white pieces to keep the look clean, modern, and sophisticated.

establish your style

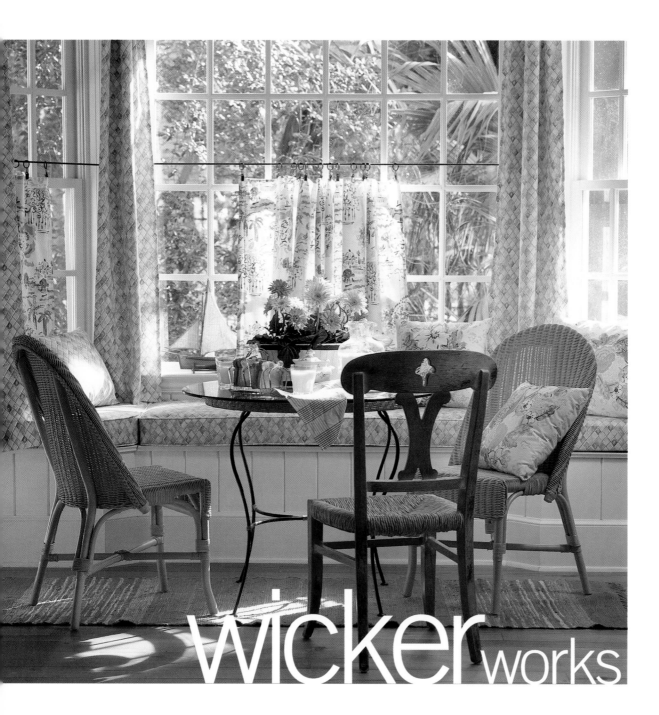

wicker works

shop the imports Superstores showcasing imported furnishings offer you style-on-a-budget pieces that will give your rooms fashionable flair and an exotic air. Turn a sleepy, barely functioning window seat into a lively breakfast area, *above,* with a variety of import-store chairs, an iron table base fitted with a glass tabletop, and lots of sew-it-yourself cushions. **collect porch chairs** from family members or find them new at import stores. Spray new chairs with several coats of paint, if desired, and tie on cushions to make stiff-backed chairs more comfortable, *opposite.* Wicker is so versatile that if you decide to upgrade to more luxurious dining chairs, you simply can move the wicker ones to other spaces.

fill in the blanks with outdoor

apples

Vegetables

Fresh Flowers

furniture

patio stores can supply you with furnishings to fill a dining room while you save for a more typical or permanent dining room set. Don't be surprised, though, if the look you create is so stylish that you toss out your earlier plans (think of the money you'll save). Here, outdoor chairs gather around a glass-topped pedestal table for a dynamic and surprising look.

a park bench Nothing beats the unexpected for a style statement. Most entry halls provide some sort of seating (when there's space) for pulling off boots and putting them on again. A park bench, *below*, is not the usual, expected piece, but you'll especially appreciate its style if you buy it for a song. Check out superstores in the spring when they display garden furniture for the coming season. Paint a bench a lively color and move it into the house. **folding chairs,** *opposite*, offer ever-versatile seating and belong in every home. You can use them everywhere, and their prices fall at the bottom of any furniture list. Superstores are notable for folding-chair selections: metal game-table chairs, wooden kitchen chairs, wood-and-metal armchairs, and stainless-steel or plastic copies of expensive dining chairs. Keep a closetful for expanding dining room seating, for pulling up to a game table, or seating a crowd on the lawn when the party grows big and lively.

more ideas Folding chairs can be found in places other than superstores. ■ For a large outdoor dinner party, rent white wooden folding chairs from a wedding-supply store. ■ Find folding church chairs in antiques malls for $8 to $10 each. ■ Lawn and garden catalogs carry affordable folding chairs—some in colorful plastics, some in wood—that can weather life outdoors.

slipCOVER it

one size fits all So you've inherited an old sofa that you can use while you save to buy a new one that expresses your true style. To disguise its weathered surface, check the home furnishings section of a superstore for a slipcover, available in standard sizes. Be sure to measure your sofa first to make sure the cover will fit.

home
center
improvements

it's the stuff of do-it-yourself **dreams**—a lumber cart filled with **off-the-rack** hardwood moldings, trims, paneling, and other **inspiring finds** for decorating your home. Try these **hands-on ideas** to take boring, boxy rooms out of their tight constraints and **free up** your decorating budget.

add depth and dimension to flat, ho-hum walls with a lattice-pattern wainscot constructed from 1×4s. Three 9-inch squares fill the area between the chair rail and baseboard in this room; you may need to construct larger or smaller squares, depending on the size of your room or how tall you want the wainscot to be. Overlap the top edge with a 1-inch chair rail molding.

stemware racks For each rack like the ones *below,* purchase two wooden brackets. Cut a 6×32-inch shelf from 1-inch-thick lumber. Three inches in from each end of the shelf and flush with the back edge, glue, clamp, and nail the brackets. Cut stemware molding (available ready-made at lumber stores) into seven 5-inch pieces. Cut a left edge from one molding piece and a right edge from another. Place these cut edges at the ends of each shelf, facing the brackets. Evenly space full molding pieces (ours are center-spaced 3¾ inches apart) flush with the back edge of the shelf. Glue and nail in place. Paint with semigloss paint. **plank paneling** To make a rustic wainscot, *opposite,* stain 1×10 red oak planks and nail them to the wall. For cottage-style paneling, install red oak planks vertically to the height of the door opening and cap them with a horizontal 1×10 nailed flush against the wall. Add wooden pegs (you'll find them in the dowel section) to the 1×10 crown. Hide the seam between the crown and the vertical planks with a strip of 1-inch quarter-round molding. For extra display space, top the 1×10 crown with a 1×10 shelf, screwed to and supported by wooden brackets. | **TO FINISH PANELING** in a soft tone, choose a pickled-oak stain. Finish the wood with the stain first; then apply the planks to the walls, filling holes with tinted surfacing compound.

instant architecture
to go

apply decoration

with wood shutters, moldings, and wallcoverings

sail-away guest room A roll or two of cloud wallcovering, *opposite,* puts a room in getaway mode. First, hang an 18-inch-wide strip of wallcovering at the ceiling. Then nail 1×3s directly onto the room's drywall surfaces to achieve a paneled look without the work and expense of true paneling. The 1×3 boards, spaced 18 inches apart, begin below the wallcovering and end above the baseboard. A 1×2 cap hides the seam between the faux paneling and the wallcovering. Special-order plantation shutters give the room movement and dimension, opening casually at the windows. **seaside mural** Check home improvement stores for ready-to-go wallcoverings. Or look in their wallcovering books for pictorial borders and coordinating wallcoverings to wrap a cottage-style bedroom. The printed designs set the tone for the whole room, so choose wisely. Plan your design so the bottom of the border aligns with the mattress top. Hang the wallcovering first; then position the border, making sure both are level with the floor. **FRAME THE BORDER with stock molding to provide definition without overwhelming the border graphics. Predrill holes and paint the stock molding. Nail it over the seams above and below the border. Fill the nail holes with wood putty and dab paint over the putty.**

paper shades are known as temporary shades in home center language. They're ready to hang by self-adhesive edges when you move into a new house. Ordinarily, they hang horizontally, but if you turn the panels sideways, they become permanent curtains with vertical pleats, *below*. To trim the shade, measure from the sill to three-fourths of the window height. Mark the length lightly across the pleats and cut, three at a time, with scissors. | **USE A PAPER PUNCH** to make holes along the edge, punching through three pleats at a time and using a previous punch as a guide. To hang the panel, insert a **36-inch-long threaded rod through the holes; the threads separate the pleats. Screw finial nuts on the rod ends and hang the rod on 2-inch eye screws.**

bifold doors make this window treatment three-dimensional. To create this effect, buy three sets of louvered bifolds, an extra hinge, three ¼-inch-diameter dowels, and 24 brass screw eyes. Separate one set of doors and use the hinges to join one door to each remaining set so it folds in the opposite direction. Remove the top rail from each door and slide the louver blades out. Use wood filler in the grooves left by the blades; let filler dry and sand smooth. Replace top rails and paint the doors. From dowels, cut 12 curtain rods ½ inch shorter than the openings. **| CUT SHEER FABRIC PANELS twice the width of the opening and 3 inches longer. Sew 1½-inch rod pockets at each end. To hang, install brass screw eyes at the tops and bottoms of the openings, 1 inch away from each side. With pliers, open the screw eyes slightly so the dowels can slip inside.**

a louvered window treatment, *below,* is one way to handle the privacy issue in a bathroom and still let the light come shining through. Mini-shuttered louvers are common items at a home center, but unless you have windows that match their measurements, you'll need to special-order your shutters. **| USE A TAPE MEASURE to determine the shutter size that will work for your window. Take the inside measurements** of your window, measure twice to be certain, and take the numbers to the home center design department. Ask the staff to help you determine the shutter size that will fit comfortably inside your window frame and allow easy opening and closing. **looking glass** illusions in a small space such as the entryway, *opposite,* add up to more light and a sense of spaciousness. To create the look, purchase louvered doors at a home center or lumberyard. Hinge them, as shown *below,* to a mirror frame you construct from 2×4 lumber. A glass dealer can cut a mirror to fit the frame size you choose. **| TO MAKE THE MIRROR FRAME,** rip 2×4 lumber to 3 inches wide, eliminating rounded edges. Cut a ½-inch rabbet ¼ inch deep to accept the mirror. To determine the size of the frame opening, place louvered doors side by side and measure their height and combined width. Make the frame opening ¼ inch taller and ⅜ inch wider than those measurements. Miter corners and assemble the frame with glue and finishing nails. Cut a hardboard back to match the overall frame dimensions. Attach a mitered-corner wood trim (the one shown is 1⅜ inches wide) around the frame with glue and brads. Prime and paint the door and frame assembly; attach the shuttered doors with 3-inch no-mortise hinges. Place the custom-cut mirror into the frame opening. Nail the hardboard back to the frame; then nail the unit to the wall, hitting studs for security.

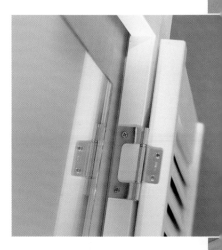

swing-arm lamps attached to the wall, *below left,* make bedtime reading easy and comfortable. Common finds in home centers, these task lamps attach to the wall with screws and simply plug into wall sockets. Even if you have space for bedside table lamps, wall-hung lights free the space for other bedroom necessities. **over-the-mirror lighting,** *below right,* is a must in every bathroom. Shop home center lighting sections for current styles to replace outdated fixtures. With the help of a lighting book, you can change the fixture yourself. Turn off the power before you begin the project. If you need better light for applying cosmetics, hang a large second mirror on the wall adjacent to the first mirror. **a pair of pendants** hung from the ceiling behind a cornice board, *opposite,* drop low over a sink area to provide ambience and a nighttime replacement for natural light. **picture lights** accent important art in a room. A clamp-on or clip-on light attaches to the top of the picture frame, *opposite below left,* and the plug-in cord, hidden behind the painting, drops to the socket below.

a combination of fixtures

works together to provide a complete lighting plan. All types—general, task, and accent—are available in the lighting sections of home improvement stores. In the dining room, *below,* a pendant light provides task lighting. Recessed lighting in the ceiling (top left in the picture) offers general lighting, and the ceiling track light (top center in the picture) accents and spotlights a prized collection in a display case.

well-lit & stylish

set do-it-yourself tile in
comfortable
patterns

vinyl tile floor

A checkerboard-style floor is an easy pattern to lay, using do-it-yourself, self-adhesive vinyl tile, *opposite*. Select the dark- and light-colored tiles right off the rack in home improvement stores, take them home, and lay a floor in a weekend. To know how much you save by installing the tile yourself, compute the home center's fee for laying the floor for you. | **PREPARE THE FLOOR** before setting the vinyl squares. Pull up the previous floor covering, remove loose or protruding nails, and sand away bumps in the subfloor. Scrub the underlayment and allow it to dry. To plan the layout, measure and mark the center of the floor. Using a T square and string, determine a straight line across floor width and length; mark the lines on the subfloor. Set your first tile on one side of the intersecting lines and work outward, filling the quadrant. Continue the process, setting each quadrant and working toward the corners of the room. Trim tiles to fit along the outer edges.

ceramic backsplash

A ceramic countertop in a green and white checkerboard pattern, *above*, continues seamlessly up the wall in a backsplash that sets the kitchen's decorative tone. The glazed tile is an easy-to-clean, hard-wearing, waterproof surface that keeps its appearance for years. Although some do-it-yourselfers can set ceramic tile successfully, the process isn't quite as simple as it seems—getting a professional finish takes a fair amount of skill. | **CHECK BOOKRACKS** in a home improvement center for a step-by-step guide if you're interested in laying ceramic tile yourself. You'll find tips on color and design, instructions on how to plan and prepare the layout, a checklist of tools and equipment, information on tiling troublesome areas (corners and around bath fixtures), and the basic steps for the entire process.

powder room charm In a small room, you can splurge on wallcovering because it's less expensive to cover a few square feet. If the wallcovering pattern darkens or crowds the space, relieve the effect with a framed mirror or two. In the tiny room *below,* removing the door of a medicine chest opened up the space. Wallpaper covers the inside of the chest where shelves once hung, and a mirror on the back wall reflects the added dimension. A small lamp on the bottom shelf adds another light source. A second mirror, hung on the adjacent wall, reflects and enhances the electrical lights in the room. **floral guest room** In a large room, *right,* covering all the walls with a printed paper can be expensive. Pattern can prove to be too much for the space, making the room feel smaller or too busy. To avoid visual crowding (and incur less expense), cover only one wall as an accent in the room. Measure the wall height and width before going to the home center to buy wallcovering; the design department can help you calculate the amount of paper to buy. In general, a standard roll of wallcovering is approximately 20½ inches × 11 yards, enough material to cover 6 square yards of wall surface.

time is money...
buy off-the-shelf papers for
instant results

mailbox posts go right to the head of the bed, *opposite top*. To make the headboard, shorten two unfinished mailbox posts to the desired height. To stabilize the posts, cut a 12-inch-wide piece of plywood the width of the bed and attach it to the posts below mattress level, using $3/4 \times 1\frac{1}{2}$-inch cleats. Drill holes in the posts to match the holes in the bed rail and attach the posts to the bed rails with bolts and washers. To fill the space between the horizontal arms, hang copper-capped fencepost tops on the wall.

picket fence perfect

To make the picket headboard, *opposite bottom,* purchase one picket fence section (panel) and bolts long enough to go through the panel and bed rail. Cut the panel to bed width; sand off rough spots as needed and paint or stain as desired. Mark the positions for the bolts on the panel to match the holes on the bed rail. Drill holes for the bolts through the panel; then fasten the headboard to the bed rail with bolts and washers. **stockade style** The light, natural pine of a stockade fence section forms a perfect backdrop for a bed dressed in natural, neutral linens, *below.* Purchase one stockade fence panel and bolts long enough to securely fasten the fence panel to the bed rail. Follow the instructions for the picket fence headboard to fasten the stockade headboard to the bed rail. Instead of painting or staining the headboard, apply a few coats of clear polyurethane varnish for a natural shine.

more ideas Add romance to a twin bed with a home center arbor kit. After you assemble the kit, cut a plywood shape to fit the back of the arbor. Staple batting and a floral sheet over the plywood and nail it to the back of the arbor. ■ Get creative with ready-made lattice panels for beds wider than arbor-kit widths. If the pieces come unpainted, add coats of primer and fresh white paint.

2nd
hand
savvy

sample

this directory of **secondhand styles** created from hand-me-downs, garage sale bargains, and flea market finds. On these **inspirational** pages, you'll also find tips for **savvy shopping** that will get you that **personal look** you want for your home.

french country Successful personal styles begin with "good bones"—
a knowledge of what you love and a sense of how you'd like your home to feel.
You can borrow a formula from history or make up the design as you go along.
Here, the homeowner adopts French styling but gives it a humorous twist.

color is key

to a mix-don't-match look

retro rustic The lipstick red table and chairs, *opposite,* priced at only $100, was too great a find for photostylist Mary Anne Thomson to pass up. It made her smile. It also inspired her happy impulse to decorate her guesthouse kitchen in 1940s restaurant style. "I've always loved vintage objects," she says, "and I found everything for this house at low prices. I wanted everything old, secondhand, like it had been in the family awhile." She mixes furniture styles freely from room to room but uses doses of red in varying amounts throughout the house to unify the overall look and color scheme.

stacked books bear titles that reveal personal interests and choices (note Mary Anne's vintage copy of *Frugal Housewife, right*). Read your books, of course, but also use them as decorative pedestals to elevate precious objects on a table.

more ideas Flea markets and outdoor antiques fairs can yield a variety of desirable objects but may be more expensive than other secondhand sources. ■ Don't overlook yard or garage sales. You may find unexpected treasures at rock-bottom prices. ■ Thrift stores, such as those operated by Salvation Army or Goodwill, also promise bargains.

THE AMERICAN FRUGAL HOUSEWIFE

collector's paradise Secondhand decorating, with its thrifty satisfactions, inspires collecting. You may think the art pottery collection, *below,* is from high-end antiques stores, but owner and inveterate junker Stephen Rutledge says, "I'm more of a garbage hound than an antiques seeker. I walk everywhere and hardly ever come home without something." He prefers haunting favorite places that have ever-changing merchandise; online auctions "are no substitute for the adventure of going out early in the morning and finding something you can't believe is available at such a low price," he says. **pure&simple** "There's something heartwarming about comfortable, old, usable things. They slow you down and make you feel peaceful and at home," says antiques dealer Lisa McCormick. She and her husband, Mark, gathered utilitarian pieces for their all-wood living room, *opposite.* Adirondack chairs, she says, are surprisingly good for lounging, especially with lots of ticking-covered pillows on them. Benches work as tables, and few keepsakes are left about to gather dust in this simple space.

prices at junk shops &
are better than those found
in antiques
stores

more ideas Here are a few rules for the secondhand-savvy road: ■ Wear comfortable shoes and dress in clothes that can stand up to a little dirt (old stuff can be dusty). Carry essentials in a backpack or hip bag so your hands are free to handle the merchandise. ■ Know yourself. It takes a special kind of confidence to choose items that truly reflect your personality. ■ Dig through instead of skimming the surface. Look under items, inside boxes and drawers. ■ When you come upon an object that attracts and intrigues you, think of unexpected ways to use it. Putting a spin on a special find will give your home more character.

garage sales

mixing formal pieces with more primitive ones produces a stylish, sophisticated comfort

cottage style "When you're furnishing on a budget, flea markets are a wonderful way to go," interior designer C.J. VanDaff says. "You start thinking of adaptive reuses—using a picnic basket for big plants to fill a corner, for example." In her den, *opposite,* C.J. uses nail barrels as side tables, a big wire basket as a magazine rack, and old shutters to wrap the room in a cozy and intimate atmosphere. Decorating with flea market finds influences C.J.'s design style: "It draws your eye to look at things in new ways, to be more creative," she says. Her advice for successful secondhand shopping? Buy what you love. Be open to possibilities but know what you can live with. Follow your impulses, but base your final price on a limit you set for yourself. **pots without lids** make wonderful vases. The sugar bowl, *above,* houses a vivacious pansy bouquet from the garden. For other lidless flowerpots, try teapots, apothecary bottles, wine bottles, and food tins.

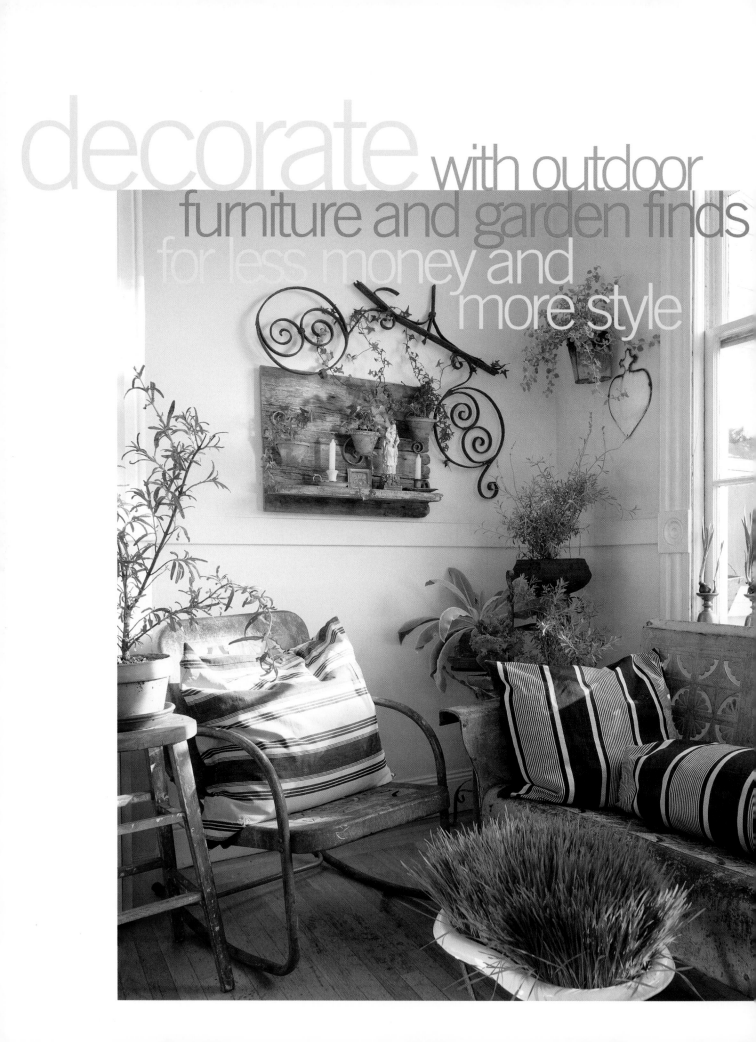

decorate with outdoor furniture and garden finds for less money and more style

gardenhouse style
Go ahead—blur the decorating boundaries between indoors and out; secondhand shopping gives you license to create new ways to live within your means. A room furnished with weathered furniture and salvaged fragments, *opposite,* is as comfortable and refreshing as a summer day. Outdoor pieces are practical too. No furniture investment can provide you with more flexibility: Pieces can move in or out, upstairs or down, and remain useful for generations to come.

gated mantel
Sometimes a secondhand outdoor element is purely aesthetic. For example, salvaged lacy grillwork and a shuttered window, *above,* serve as artwork in a room with fine furnishings. The arrangement proves that you can pair the rustic with the refined and still create a supremely stylish room.

more ideas Once you've found something you like at a sale, evaluate its condition. ■ A little rust on metal or peeling paint on wood adds charm, but if small children frequent your home, avoid pieces with flaking paint (the paint is dangerous if ingested). ■ If pieces are missing from your find, assess the expense of replacing them or decide whether you can live with the object as it is.

european flavor Barbara Novogratz cruises

European flea markets, notepad in hand, finding treasures for
her shop and her home. It's a useful habit she developed as
a young military wife. The notepad, she says, is for negotiation.
When she sees a piece she wants, she asks the dealer to write
down a price on her notepad. Then calculating the exchange
rate in her head, Barbara writes down a counteroffer. She
cautions, "Be careful when you make an offer in Paris. If it's
too low, you may insult the vendors, and they won't sell to you
at any price." Back in the United States, Barbara incorporates
her flea market finds in her home. An overmantel on the wall
in the bedroom, *right,* serves as a display shelf; the prize
painted bed charges the room with old-world style and inspires
linens of frilly lace, handmade embroidery, and patchwork.

a garden chair, *below,* finds new life inside the
house, where it serves up fluffy white towels in a bathroom.
Next year, it may find its way to another room.

more ideas If you like, make haggling a part of your purchase.
■ Politely asking for a better price usually prompts the dealer
to take 5 to 10 percent off the marked price. If the price is
marked "firm," don't haggle. ■ To make a counteroffer, avoid
going drastically lower, especially if the price is reasonable.

all you need to know
to shop euro-flea:
learn the exchange rate
and how to say thank you

use strong jolts of color sparingly as accents on clean & light backgrounds

modern country Pamela Fritz likes everything rustic, but her decorating approach is decidedly modern. "I use natural fabrics," she says. "Everything is scaled down and scaled back, with light colors and no clutter. Everything looks lived in." Generous amounts of white paint and white fabrics, combined with rusty elements, are key to the modern look. Sap cans in assorted sizes and colors hang on a living room wall, *left,* to create a contemporary-style, real-object painting. **ticktock,** times gone by. Secondhand finds, especially French ones, provide Pamela's rooms with vintage character and a look of age, connecting her to a long-ago, magical past. The late-19th-century clock face, *below,* hangs above a workbench. A pair of 1930s bowls, working together as a single jolt of red, is part of the uncluttered arrangement.

xture makes the difference between a well-designed room and one that resonates richness

country in the city Secondhand chairs and tables surround a new upholstered sofa. Fresh white mats frame old prints, and dark, nubby surfaces contrast with smooth, light finishes. Although neutral in color, opposing textures make the room interesting. The pairing of opposites is a lesson worth taking to any room you decorate.

decor by the yard

stitches
in time

save decorating dollars. **Fabrics infuse** a room with spirit, giving it softened edges, texture, and pattern. For **fabric style** by the yard, try some of the **sew-it-yourself** ideas on the following pages. You'll also find **no-sew tips** for decorating with fabrics.

muslin and canvas are at the top of the list for creating low-cost style. In spite of their humble prices and plainness, they have an elegant look when paired with white paints and natural surfaces. Use fabric-store patterns to sew window blinds or a piped skirt for a round decorator table.

piped pillows add a dash of colorful tailoring to a fabric-snappy room, *above*. Taking a cue from the chartreuse trim on the sofa, the homeowner stitched piping of a similar hue into brightly colored, knife-edge sofa pillows. To make a pillow, purchase a pillow form, contrasting fabrics, and cotton cording. | **CUT A PILLOW FRONT** and back, allowing for 1-inch seams. From contrasting fabric, cut 2-inch-wide strips on the bias (diagonal) for piping. Join the strips end to end, making a continuous length to fit the pillow perimeter. With wrong sides facing, fold the piping strip in half lengthwise over the cording. Use a zipper foot to stitch close to the cord; sew piping to the pillow front along the seam line. To join the piping ends, stop stitching 2 inches before the end. Trim cord ends to meet, leaving a ½-inch overlap of fabric. Wrap fabric around cord ends; stitch across the join. Stitch the pillow front to the pillow back, leaving an opening for turning. Turn pillow cover right side out, insert pillow form, and sew closed. **two-tone panels** *center,* hang from curtain rods fastened to

the wall just below a crown molding. To make fan-pleated headers like these, use 3¼-inch-wide triple-pleat tape. When you pull the pleating tape cords, the tape forms fans of triple pleats evenly spaced along the curtain top. For fabric, measure twice the track, pole, or rod length.

CUT 22-INCH-LONG PIECES for the upper sections of the panels; if your walls are 8 feet high, cut 75-inch-long lower sections from a second fabric. With flat-fell seams, fasten the two sections together. Hem the sides of each panel with 2-inch-wide hems. Add the pleating tape at the top, following the manufacturer's instructions; hand-sew curtain rings to the centers of the pleats. Hang the panels on the rod to measure for hems; finish with 3-inch-wide hems.

no-sew lace panels form a romantic window treatment, *above*. Made from curtains or tablecloths purchased at yard sales, they can be draped over a curtain rod. To give the panels a curve, mount a wooden finial on one side of the window frame at the middle or sash level; gather up the lace and loop it over the finial.

parsons chairs are so classic that fabric store pattern books offer patterns for slipcovering them. Check the home decor sections of pattern books for the slipcovers; also check for correct yardages to purchase. The slipcovers here were created from a variety of fabrics—vintage bark cloth drapery panels and solid-color coordinating fabrics. The bark cloth on the chair backs creates visual impact. For the same effect, choose a patterned fabric with a design that will draw attention to the flat back of the chair.

slipcover a classic chair

double the pleasure
with coordinated prints

totally toile In the game of contrasts, complementary hues, such as red and green, are hands-down winners because of the energy they create in a room. Raspberry and lime green (color-wheel opposites) join forces on lined curtains, *opposite,* reversing and conversing in a lively exchange of related prints. Some textile manufacturers coordinate colors and patterns for you; check the decorator section of your local fabric store. If the store doesn't stock what you want, you can select and order coordinating prints from swatch books. Some stores provide large samples that you can check out and take home to view. | **SEW TWO 52-INCH-WIDE PANELS** back to back for each side of the curtain. Edge with 2-inch-wide checked borders on the sides and bottom. Trim to the desired length and top with a 2-inch-wide rod pocket. Slip the panels onto a mounted curtain rod and pin the panels to the sides of the window frame to show off the underside print. **picture pillow** Pull out a single image from a repeated fabric pattern to display on a pillow front, *above.*

| **DETERMINE THE PILLOW SIZE** by separating one image from the larger printed pattern (lay sheets of white paper around it until the motif or picture is clearly defined). Allow for 1-inch seams on all sides and cut out the pillow front. Cut a pillow back from a coordinating print. Cut bias strips for piping from checked fabric (see page 96 for details on making piping). Sew the piping to the pillow front along the seam lines. With right sides facing, sew the pillow back to the pillow front, leaving an opening for turning. Turn the pillow cover right side out, fill it with polyester or down, and sew the opening closed.

flea market finds meet fashion fabrics

mix old and new Any fabric can come into decorative play, provided it's in good condition and carries the attitude you crave. Besides a consistent color scheme, the secret to mixing and matching fabrics is scale. For the simplest way to mix fabrics, select a showcase print (midsize vintage florals in this room). Coordinate it with a larger-scale stripe and plaid in the same colors (new sheets and pillowcases). Then add another floral print in the same large scale but with a different background color (the green floral comforter).

hooking the eye A room with a view isn't always desirable, especially if the window is small and the view less than ideal. Folds of shimmery sheer fabric, *right,* tinted to reflect a room's palette, can mask either problem while bringing dimension to a flat wall. **USE A ROW OF IRON HOOKS** instead of a curtain rod, fastening them to the wall every 6 to 8 inches. Roll-hem all edges of two 84-inch-long fabric panels. On the top of each panel, sew long ribbon ties at the ends and centers. Then sew ties at even intervals between the end and center ties. Tie the ribbons around the hooks on the wall.

luxurious length, not costly fabric, creates the unlined, light-diffusing curtains, *opposite.* Rubber O-rings softly gather the tops of muslin panels. To determine the amount of yardage to buy, measure the wall from the ceiling to the floor and add about 12 inches. Measure the width of the window and multiply by 2½. Cut fabric panels to the desired length, piecing them together at the sides to achieve the desired width. Roll-hem all raw edges.

MARK THE TOP EDGE of each curtain at even intervals, about 24 inches apart. Pinch the fabric between your fingers at the first mark. Lift the fabric and, with the fingers of your other hand, compress the fabric about 9 inches below the mark. Fold the 9-inch-length in half; slip a rubber O-ring over the top fold and down about 1½ inches. Repeat across the top. Place S hooks over a mounted rod. Slip the fabric loops over the ends of the S hooks. Arrange the curtain ends gracefully on the floor.

upholstery fabrics can take up a large part of your decorating budget, so choose coverings that are suitable for their purposes. Upholstered seating comes with either fitted, tacked-down covers or separately sewn slipcovers. Fitted covers have a finished, formal look and are usually cheaper than slipcovers; however, they can't be removed for cleaning. Because fitted covers are under constant tension, they must be of extra-durable fabric. If you're purchasing fabric to cover a chair, check labels for upholstery suitability. If you have any doubts, ask before you buy. If your new sofa or chair hasn't been treated with stain repellent, do it yourself. Although they cost more initially, slipcovers are easy to remove for cleaning or a decorative change. If you're considering a sofa with slipcovers, find out how much a spare set will cost; some retailers offer them periodically as a sales incentive. To prevent shrinking, many slipcovers come with a dry-cleaning recommendation. If the fabric is washable cotton or linen, the covers may withstand laundering in a washing machine in cool water. Put them back on the sofa while they're still slightly damp to stretch and dry in place. If you feel unsure about the outcome of this cleaning method, try a single cushion cover first.

CHOOSE NEUTRAL COLORS, contrasting textures, and low-key patterns for a unified look. Ivory paint transforms a once dark, cramped room into a light and cheerful space, *opposite*. Cream-colored fabrics with varying textures and subtle prints continue the neutral color scheme. Preshrunk canvas slipcovers can be machine washed for easy cleaning.

make careful choices for upholstery

penny
wise
details

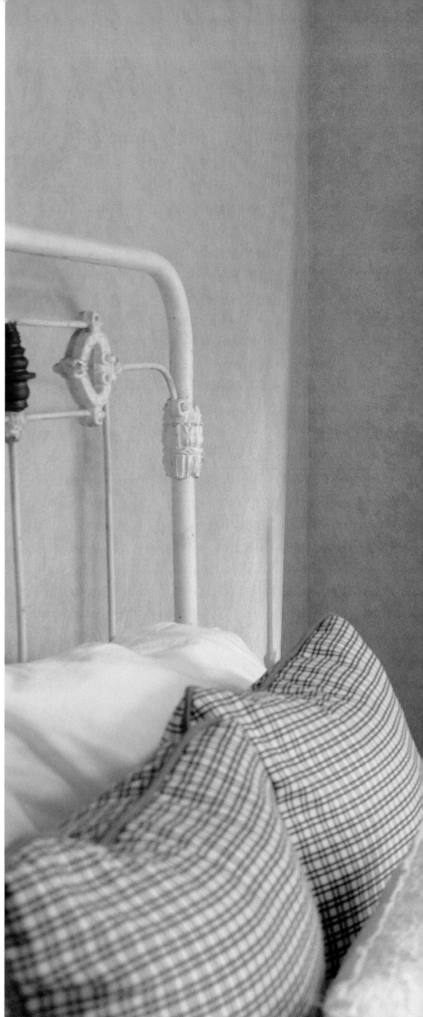

borrow

stylists' secrets from the pages of **decorating books** and magazines. One photo is worth **a thousand decorating lessons!** Here's a sampling of **inexpensive** and **valuable** accessory-**arranging tips** from decorating pros.

"I love the change of seasons," says garden writer Elvin McDonald. "It forces you to change, and change is stimulating." With a pretty pair of floral-print curtain panels (hung from a rod fastened on the wall), he creates a guest room "window" to celebrate spring and summer.

"Bring order and beauty to a kitchen with a clear-out-the-clutter plan," advises photostylist Matthew Mead. First, remove barely used items from the counter. Then sort countertop must-haves by function and organize them in containers. Arrange distinctive bowls and platters on easy-to-reach open shelving, where they'll also serve as art. Edit your collection to create a balanced composition, and limit the color scheme to one or two colors; add interest with a variety of shapes. Position the largest items first for a backdrop, then layer medium-size objects in front so the arrangement has depth. Overlap pieces to lead the eye across the display, but remember to leave a little "negative space" (empty space) between some items so the grouping doesn't look crowded. **kitchen vases** come in all sorts of disguises. Check your cupboards for watertight containers. Put small flowers in clear glasses and pretty cups. Consider pitchers and large bowls for a larger bouquet. An upright pottery canister, *below,* holds a tall, loose bundle of garden flowers. If the container isn't watertight, insert a plastic or glass liner to hold the flowers.

display
utilitarian objects as art

create
a focal point

exaggerate the size of picture mats to make impressive displays of small prints. That's what stylist Becky Jerdee did to change an ordinary wall into a focal point, *opposite.* "You'll get a big bang for your buck with do-it-yourself frames, large white mats, and black and white prints from old magazines," she says. To make an informal picture group, select three small prints with a common theme and similar coloration. Vary the mat and frame sizes so that one piece is noticeably larger than the other two. To arrange them on a picture rail, place the largest picture to one side and counterbalance it with the next largest frame. Then place the smallest piece on a table easel in front of the rail. Adjust the pictures along the rail behind the easel picture until you sense that the positions and spaces around them are balanced. "Arranging is mostly an intuitive process," Becky says. "Trust yourself to know when things are right." **get the picture** In the absence of an expensive headboard, *below,* hang a large art poster in a do-it-yourself frame to create drama and inspire color for the rest of the room.

repeat for effect

more means more style when similar shapes are massed together in a stunning display like the one *above*. The grouping is pleasing instead of chaotic because all the pieces have one thing in common: the color white. Subtle patterning—slight variations around the plate edges—adds visual interest. Rectangular frames provide a contrasting element within the display to give it structure and balance. Without these pieces, the round items would have "rolled" around on the wall begging for something to stabilize them. The symmetry of the entire display gives the arrangement a formal, solid, and comfortable look. **choose a theme** Designer Linda Westbury suggests choosing a theme for an arrangement of pictures. "Choose all wood frames or similar-style prints," she says, "to hold the thought and create gathering points." Generous mats with frames that almost touch make a cozy arrangement on her wall, *opposite*. Oval frames and rounded shapes on the table soften and contrast with all the right angles of the wall display.

cozy a corner in an oversize room. If you've just purchased a new home with large rooms, you may be wondering how to fill all those big, empty spaces with what little money you have left. Take one step at a time and start in a corner. A folding screen behind the sofa, *opposite,* turns a blank corner into a colorful backdrop for a mix of seating. A trompe l'oeil wallcovering on the screen creates an instant library. **"divide and conquer"** is an apt way to describe what's at work in the entryway, *above.* The phrase usually applies to ways of arranging furniture in long, narrow rooms; here the space is divided for beauty's sake. A folding screen in a closet-less entry hides the clutter of coats and boots at the end of an otherwise warm and welcoming space. If your front door opens into the living room, use a folding screen to divide space and create an entry.

more ideas Accessories convey comfort and warmth. Try these budget-conscious warm-ups: ■ Cluster candles in an empty fireplace, in a dreary corner, or on a tabletop. ■ Add warmth to blank white walls with simple wall hangings, such as frameless posters, tapestry remnants, or a favorite quilt on a wall-hung rod.
■ Fill an empty spot at the top of the stairs with a tabletop gallery of family photos.

create a focal point in a massed arrangement. A mirror set to the side of an arrangement, *above,* is a natural nucleus for the cluster of photographs above the bathroom shelf. Familiar faces in frames hang from a curtain rod fastened on the wall, keeping clutter off the shelf. Breathing-room spaces are allowed between objects.

group similar objects You can't go wrong if you choose items that share the same color and material. Green glassware filled with baby's breath and Queen Anne's lace, *left,* creates a mini-meadow in a kitchen window. Vary the glassware heights, from low jars to tall bottles. Arrange the containers in overlapping triangles to create a sense of movement and stagger pieces from front to back to give the grouping depth. **start with a collection** to develop a decorating scheme. Chintzware, *opposite,* determined the plan for a floral approach in the living room. Varied in scale, the flowered patterns play the lead role. Plaid fabrics and framed photographs insert opposing, rectangular shapes for contrast and balance.

more ideas Have fun and build your decorating confidence by playing with the above principles of display in small ways. ■ Create a new tabletop arrangement with your favorite reads, a sentimental object, and a large tray. ■ Arrange a wall shelf with white pitchers and hang a favorite picture below the shelf. ■ Mass a bouquet of flowers in a lidless pot.

mass for impact

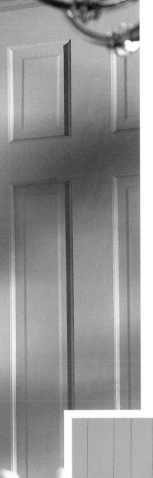

"Don't worry about matching fabric colors and patterns. Concentrate on a good blend," designer Paulette Domercq advised when styling her sister Carolyn's new kitchen, *opposite*. This attitude toward decorating helped Paulette integrate a fruit-pattern table skirt, rainbow-plaid chair seats, and an area rug from Carolyn's previous home. To get the look of real plates hanging on the wall behind the actual plates on the rack, Paulette purchased extra wallpaper and worked closely with the installer to cut and paste it correctly. She used the wedgwood blue in the wallpaper as a guide for selecting paint for the kitchen cabinetry and breakfast room doors. **display blue and white** plates on pale yellow walls for a sunshine-fresh, spring garden look, *below*. Although you may think of yellow as soft and pale, it can become a strong color in large doses. Before you select a yellow paint for several walls in your home, buy up to three test quarts to paint on large paper sheets. Hang the paper on a wall to see what effect the color will have in the room. In general, your final selection probably will be paler than the one you chose first.

think
outside the box

use ordinary objects for unusual purposes. A new use for a vintage find may occur to you immediately, but if it doesn't, be patient and let its function evolve. Stacked OshKosh suitcases, *opposite,* serve as a side table—and as storage space for winter clothes. **see containers for what they aren't** A corn planter in its original red paint, *left,* works well as a wall-hung vase for flowers. Other ideas to try: Use a new aluminum tool chest made for pickup trucks (you can buy them at home improvement centers) for end-of-the-bed storage. Turn a wall-mount kitchen cabinet on its side to use as a table and bookcase, or cut an old oil drum in half to make a coffee table base for a glass tabletop. **turn it upside down or sideways** A section of flower-bed fencing holds towels and kitchen utensils, *below,* while cast-iron bathtub feet (turned upside down) make heavy bookends.

more ideas Storage doesn't have to mean straight-lined boxes and drawers. Experiment with off-the-wall ideas. ■ Turn the top half of an antique washstand upside down and hang it on the wall for a shapely quilt rack. ■ Turn an old picture frame into a vanity tray by fitting it with a mirror. ■ Serve up bath soaps in a silver pastry rack and fresh towels in a soup tureen.

trim a bedroom "The deliciousness of decorating with white lies in its simplicity, its timeless perfection, and its tremendous breadth of tones," says writer Lisa Kingsley. "White is not one color, but many. When it comes to mixing whites, be fearless." In the bedroom, *above,* creamy white upholstery pieces sit comfortably next to pure white linens. **paint a backdrop** of white to give a room open, airy spaces. In spite of humble, budget furniture, the all-white room, *right,* conveys a lighthearted, simple, yet elegant attitude. A pale green and white striped wallcovering on the wardrobe doors and walls keeps the room from looking like a winter snowstorm. **starch it** Crisp white chair aprons, *opposite,* are budget-conscious handmade slips of cotton tied to the chair seats. To sew them, make a pattern: Cover a chair seat with a large sheet of paper and crease the paper at the edges of the chair to make an imprint. Pencil in the desired drops on the front and sides; add seam allowances and cut out the pattern. Pin it to a double layer of white fabric; cut out. Sew the fabric pieces together, leaving an opening for turning. Turn right side out and add long, narrow ties.

apply white for
elegance

tree branches in an outdoor room, *right,* are free and mirror nature. All you need is a tree that's agreeable to cutting; the rest is easy. Use plant-hanging hooks to fasten the branch curtain rods to a ceiling or window frame. Then tie spaghetti-strap curtains from the central section of the branch. Note the simple (and free) stone anchor that keeps the panel from blowing about in the wind. **drawer pulls** from a hardware store or home improvement center hold the curtain panel, *below.* Because the knobs must be secured from the back, cut a board the width of the window frame and paint it to match the frame. Drill through the board to attach the knobs, spacing them 7 inches apart. Mount the board over the window frame.

hanging style for pennies

the scarf onto the rod the way you pin sheets on a clothesline. **stick pins** are made especially for hanging flat panels. You'll find them in drapery stores, window hardware and home furnishings catalogs, and import and discount stores. Find a lace panel or sheer scarf that's slightly larger than your window frame. At the top, push a pin through each corner of the panel and into the window frame. Sweep a bottom corner to the window sash on the opposite side and pin it to the frame.

shaker pegs are available at home centers in the dowel section of the store. To hang a curtain valance like the one *above,* drill ⅜-inch-deep holes in the window frame (it will be a permanent installation, so be sure this is definitely the hanging style you want). Space the holes about 6 inches apart. Use wood glue to fasten the ends of the pegs in place. Then tie on a valance or full-length curtain panel. **office clips** Cool accessories needn't be expensive. The drapery hardware, *opposite bottom right,* is actually a threaded rod from a hardware store and hinged clips from an office supply store. Threaded rods come in standard lengths of 36 inches, but you can have the hardware store cut them to fit your window. Slide a ready-made sheer curtain panel on the rod and fasten the rod to the window frame with screw hooks. The clip fastener is ideal for hanging a fashion scarf as an overlay curtain. Clip

style on a budget tool kit

practical

decorating strategies that **save money** almost always include doing some of the work yourself. In this chapter you'll find a list of **helpful tools**, ideas for creating **a style file**, and a handy **room-arranging kit** for planning your style-on-a-budget home.

plan your rooms by layers Think of each room as a theater set for staging your life. Each room has three parts: a backdrop of dramatic or not-so-dramatic walls and floors; furniture, the building blocks for comfortable living; and accessories or "props"—lamps, pictures, pillows— that express your signature style.

decorator's tool kit

tool glossary So you're the budget-conscious type who likes to save decorating expenses by doing projects yourself. Any project is easier to accomplish if you have the right tools. Here are some basic supplies to keep on hand.

awl An awl, which resembles an ice pick, lets you make a starter hole or pilot hole in wood so nails and screws go in more easily.

can opener You'll need this to open a can of paint. Sometimes you can get one free with the purchase of paint. Pick up paint sticks for stirring too.

carpenter's level Don't try to "eyeball" it. Make sure your project is level by resting this tool along the surface. The bubble will be centered in the vial when the item is level. An aluminum level doubles as a straightedge for cutting.

caulk Choose a paintable acrylic or acrylic combination for indoor surfaces. It's used for sealing around bathtubs, sinks, and windows as well as for filling gaps between baseboard or crown molding and the wall.

clamps To hold objects together while you work on them or while glue sets, choose multipurpose C-clamps. Use pads when clamping wood to avoid damaging the surface.

crafts knife Check crafts stores for retractable single-blade knives and replacement blades. To get a clean cut when cutting thick materials such as mat board or foam-core board, use a new blade.

electric drill This tool is indispensable. A ¼- or ⅜-inch drill will handle most home decorating projects. Look for a reversible drill with variable speed control. A screwdriver bit makes quick work of installing valances, shelves, and cornices. Cordless drills are convenient if your project isn't near an electrical outlet.

fabric shears These scissors are made for (and should be reserved for) cutting fabric.

floral shears Scissors for cutting flower stems come with notched blades to provide extra leverage when cutting stems and ribbon for floral bouquets. Some shears can be taken apart for easy cleaning by hand or in the dishwasher.

glues Stock up on a variety of adhesives. For gluing fabrics, check crafts and fabric stores for washable fabric glues. For general purpose gluing of porous surfaces such as wood and paper, thick white crafts glue works well. For gluing wood to wood, use carpenter's glue. Five-minute epoxy also is recommended for adhering wood to wood, as well as for gluing nonporous surfaces such as metals, glass, porcelain, tile, and plastic.

grommet tool This tool, which is sold in fabric stores, is designed to press together the two halves of a grommet or eyelet, enclosing the fabric between them and making holes for lacing or threading.

hammer A 16-ounce claw hammer is a good all-purpose tool. The claw provides leverage for pulling nails and removing crooked ones from lumber.

handsaw Quality counts here—an inexpensive saw can chew up your wood and ruin a project. With an 8- to 10-point crosscut saw, you can cut across the grain of the wood, the most common type of sawing. (The points refer to the number of teeth per inch.) A backsaw is a type of crosscut saw with finer teeth (12 to 13 points per inch) for cutting miters. Keep saws covered with a sheath or cardboard when not in use.

hot-glue gun Every do-it-yourselfer needs at least one hot-glue gun. High-temperature glue produces the strongest bond and won't soften when exposed to sunlight or heat, but the glue can burn your skin and damage some fabrics and plastics. Low-temperature glues are less likely to burn skin or fabric, but the glue tends to soften in high-heat areas or in direct sunlight. For greatest versatility, choose a dual-temperature gun that can accept both types of glue sticks; also look for models with built-in safety stands.

paintbrushes Choose good-quality natural- or synthetic-bristle brushes for major painting projects. For small jobs or for use with acrylic crafts paints, inexpensive foam brushes work well and are disposable.

painter's tape This low-tack masking tape leaves no residue after removal. Use it to mask off areas where you don't want paint to go while you're painting an adjacent area.

pliers The two basic types you need to have on hand are slip-joint pliers and needle-nose pliers.

plumb bob Available at hardware stores, this tool is a cord with a pointed weight at one end; it's used to determine whether a vertical line is perpendicular. To use it, attach the end of the cord to the ceiling, suspending the weight just above the floor.

safety goggles Always wear goggles when scrubbing with a heavy-duty cleaner, sanding wood, using furniture stripper, or painting a ceiling.

sandpaper Keep an assortment of coarse, medium, and fine grits on hand to use on raw wood, between paint coats, or after a final coat of varnish.

scrapers Scrapers and putty knives come in different widths for different jobs: removing old paint, wallpaper, varnish, or glue or applying surfacing compound. Keep them clean and sharpen them often.

screwdriver For the best quality, look for cushioned, easy-grip handles and fracture-resistant bars and tips. You'll need both standard and phillips screwdrivers with tips in a variety of sizes.

sewing needles and pins Keep on hand a box of dressmaker's pins, an assortment of sewing needles, and a package of heavy-duty large-eye or tapestry needles. Quilter's pins also are good for upholstery fabrics, because they're extra long and have large plastic heads that are easy to see. T pins are heavy, T-shape pins used for temporarily securing fabric to an upholstered piece.

staple gun This is a must for stapling fabric to a chair seat or to a wood strip (for window swags). Look for one that lets you push down at the front where the staple comes out so you'll have leverage.

stud sensor If you're hanging bed canopies, window boxes, mirrors, or shelves, you'll be glad you have one of these. Electronic versions flash and beep when they locate studs, joists, and other objects; the sensor even works through extra-thick walls and floors.

tack cloth Check hardware stores for this loosely woven cloth that has been treated to make it slightly sticky so it picks up sanding dust.

tape measure For sewing projects, you'll need a flexible plastic or cloth tape with a metal end. For woodworking projects, a heavy-duty retractable metal tape is helpful; the end of the tape hooks over a door frame, a window frame, or the end of a piece of wood to hold the tape in place.

window scraper With a single-edge razor holder, you can scrape paint from windows or remove sticky labels from glass.

wire cutter This clipper-like tool is handy for cutting mirror- and picture-hanging wire.

storing your tools A designated storage unit for your tools will save you both time and money—hunting down tools is a waste of time that may result in a second purchase that duplicates something you already have but can't find. If the traditional carpenter's tool chest, fishing tackle box, or antique wooden tool carrier doesn't suit your personal style, try one of these creative tool-storage ideas:

1 Look for canvas tool bags at home centers. Or adapt a hanging canvas clothes holder or a clear vinyl hanging shoe bag. Small- to medium-size tools slip in and out of cubbyholes or shoe slots and are easy to see. If you buy a plastic one, make sure the plastic is heavy and sturdy so sharp objects won't pierce it.

2 Stackable plastic bins or trays are other storage options. If you like to carry your tools with you, use a duffel bag or picnic basket. Small, often-used tools can be kept neatly in a cosmetics bag. Or check hardware stores and discount variety stores for specialty tool organizers that incorporate pockets of various sizes, stackable trays, and a step stool or bucket.

3 Assemble a decorating closet, a space designated to hold practical hammer-and-nail supplies as well as more creative ones, such as flower vases, candles, or party decorations. It could be a closet at the end of a hall, open shelving in the basement, an armoire with basket containers, a large trunk at the end of a bed, or a space behind a folding screen.

creating a style file Many hands-on, do-it-yourself decorators clip and save magazine pictures of rooms to inspire their future decorating projects—or at least to move them one step closer to getting around to a project someday. Like glimpses from a diary or journal, these icons of decorating dreams reveal composite pictures of your personal, evolving style. If you haven't practiced the clip-and-save habit or organized the bits and pieces of your decorating desires, it's a rewarding and confidence-building exercise to make a portrait of your decorating self. Here are some things you can do to start:

1 Tear out magazine pages that inspire you to do what you see in the pictures. As you collect the pages, you'll begin to see themes and color schemes develop; you'll note your tastes in certain styles of furniture. Be discriminating about what you tear out, so you'll avoid cluttering your decorating portrait with marginal ideas. Be decisive about your choices; nobody's looking or

judging, so you can be clear about who you are as a decorator. Remember that your choices needn't lock you in. As you evolve, you can change your mind about what you love. Assemble the pictures and tear sheets on scrapbook pages, in pocketed folders, or in file drawers. A scrapbook documents your evolving story in a more permanent fashion than pocketed folders or files. If you prefer something you can easily clean out from time to time, choose folders or file drawers.

2 Document your color style. Stand in front of a paint store color-card rack and clear your mind of all past paint and decorating experiences. Disconnect from fashion or clothing color choices and let your hand go where your heart leads it. Choose the color that attracts you most. Call it your signature color. From the display, choose a second color that works with your signature color; pick a third. Then go to a home center paint rack and repeat the exercise, exploring warm and cool variations of your signature color and collecting a few more color chips for your style file.

3 Collect print images that inspire you. They can come from anywhere—a wonderful matchbox, a picture postcard, the image on a program cover, anything that appeals to you. Tuck them in your files next to your colors and tearsheets.

4 Tap your memory for decorating inspirations. Remember the rooms of your childhood that welcomed you home and visualize those that compelled you to linger. On paper, list the furnishings and colors present in those rooms. They may be comfort symbols and clues to your style. If you have a natural affinity for family furnishings, draw upon that as part of your style.

5 Map out a decorating plan. Call it "decorating in stages" and begin with good foundation pieces: a sofa, a concert grand, a pair of upholstered chairs. In words or pictures, envision how (over a period of months or years) you'll make changes that will move you toward a completed scheme. You may not have the means to accomplish it just yet, but visualizing future plans is an exercise that builds your decorative muscle.

6 Give your style a name. If you're having trouble describing or applying a label to your inherent style (country, traditional, contemporary), try this: On a piece of paper, list your colors, the style of furnishings you prefer, and your favorite collectibles. Consider what theme or characteristics they have in common. Then find words to give your theme a name. Say, for example, you love white wicker, clear blues and greens for walls and fabrics, and collections of seashells and folk art.

You might name your style Beach Style. Identifying your decorating personality with a label gives you confidence and helps you focus your look.

arranging furniture
An inviting room has less to do with what you have than with how you use what you have. Follow these guidelines to design a room from scratch or rearrange your furnishings to make the most of your space.

1 Direct traffic. If traffic passes through a room, it doesn't have to run through the center of it. Think of your furniture pieces as walls or guideposts that can funnel traffic around your conversation area.

2 Float furnishings. A lineup of furniture around a room is about as cozy as a waiting room. Pull pieces away from walls into close-knit groupings, with major seating pieces no more than 8 feet apart.

3 Keep convenience within reach. Set a handy resting place for drinks or books close to every seat. It can be a true end table, a stack of books, or a piece of glass atop a decorative basket or cube. The items should be stable and the surface roughly the same height as the arm of the chair or sofa next to it.

4 Do a balancing act. Combine furnishings of different heights and hefts for interest, but avoid placing all your tall or weighty pieces on the same side of the room; otherwise, the room will look lopsided.

5 Forget room labels. Use space creatively, letting your furniture determine the room's function. Who says your L-shape dining area can't function as a TV spot? Why not dine in the living room?

6 Try a fresh angle. Because a diagonal is the longest line through any room, an angled grouping creates an illusion of width. On-the-bias seating also takes advantage of two focal points—for example, a fireplace and window view—at once. In a long, narrow room, placing furniture on the diagonal helps break a skinny room into a friendlier time-out spot.

7 Cozy up a big room. Divide and conquer. Break the room into two or more furniture groupings for coziness and better function.

8 Maximize a small room. Include a large-scale piece, such as a vintage armoire or an ample love seat, for a feeling of grandeur. Use vertical storage in tight spaces.

9 Fix low or high ceilings. "Raise" a low ceiling with floor-to-ceiling window treatments and tall furniture. "Lower" a ceiling with a colorful area rug and table lamps, which bring light lower; play up the floor-hugging look by hanging artwork so that it's at eye level when you are seated.

furniture arranging
on paper

when planning your room schemes on paper, use the symbols here and on the following pages to profile your spaces and visualize them with more dimension. Here's how to use the paper kit:

1 Copy pages 138–141 on a black and white copy machine at a local copy shop. Make several copies of the graph paper for different scenarios. Or on plain paper, trace only the templates that best reflect your furnishings. Then use the graph on pages 142–143 to begin experimenting with different arrangements.

2 Measure your room. Plot it on the grid, using one square per square foot of floor space. Determine the length of each wall and draw it onto the floor plan. Mark windows with a double line, leave an open area for doorways, and indicate door swings. Include architectural features such as fireplaces, sliding glass doors, and stairways.

3 Measure your present furniture pieces or the new ones you plan to purchase. Match them to the corresponding kit symbols and cut out the templates.

4 Find a focal point. Physically, this is the cornerstone around which you'll group your furnishings; visually, it's the dramatic element that draws you into a room. If your room doesn't have a natural focus—a fireplace, built-in bookcases, or an expansive window—substitute a large-scale or boldly colored accessory or use freestanding wall units.

5 Once you've found the focus, arrange your furniture templates on the graph-paper floor plan. Keep the furniture-arranging tips, *page 136,* in mind as you reposition the pieces.

6 When you arrive at an arrangement you'd like to save for future reference, tape down the pieces with transparent tape and tuck the plan into your style file.

architectural symbols

STAIR

DOUBLE DOOR

RADIATOR

COVERED RADIATOR

DOUBLE HUNG SASH

CASEMENT SASH OPENING IN OR OUT

DOOR SWINGING IN OR OUT

BIFOLD DOORS

SLIDING DOORS - 6 or 8 FT.

CASED OPENING (PASSAGE)

FIREPLACE WITH MANTEL

electrical symbols

$ LIGHT OR OTHER SWITCH

LIGHT FIXTURE (Not Lamp)

SINGLE-POLE SWITCH

3-WAY SWITCH

DUPLEX OUTLET

TV ANTENNA OUTLET

AIR-CONDITIONING (20 amp.) OUTLET

FLOOR OUTLET

TELEPHONE

CEILING FAN

BELL

incandescent light outlets

RECESSED CEILING

WALL BRACKET

CEILING

TRACK LIGHTING

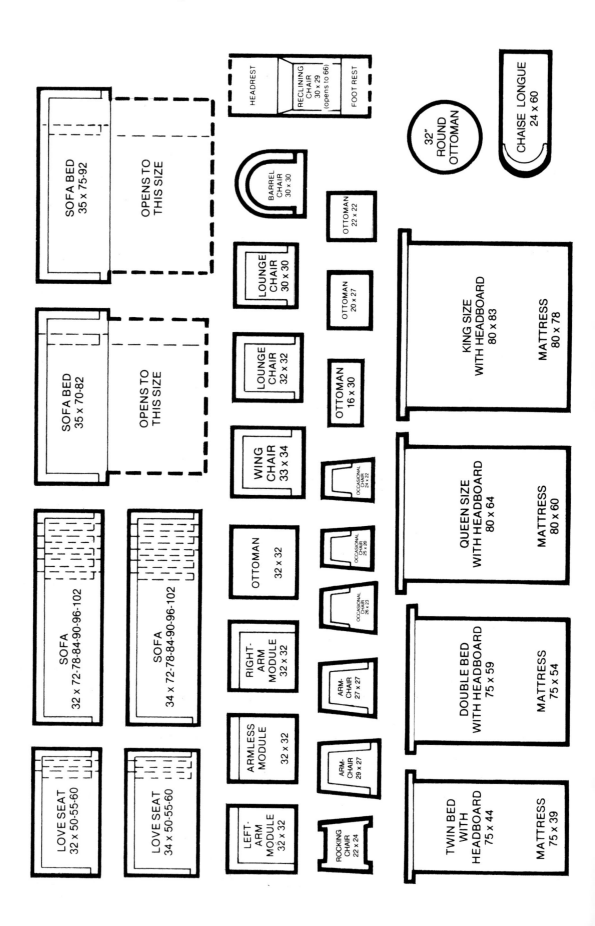

SOFA BED
35 x 75-92

OPENS TO
THIS SIZE

SOFA BED
35 x 70-82

OPENS TO
THIS SIZE

SOFA
32 x 72-78-84-90-96-102

SOFA
34 x 72-78-84-90-96-102

LOVE SEAT
32 x 50-55-60

LOVE SEAT
34 x 50-55-60

HEADREST

RECLINING
CHAIR
30 x 29
(opens to 66)

FOOT REST

BARREL
CHAIR
30 x 30

LOUNGE
CHAIR
30 x 30

LOUNGE
CHAIR
32 x 32

WING
CHAIR
33 x 34

OTTOMAN
32 x 32

RIGHT-
ARM
MODULE
32 x 32

ARMLESS
MODULE
32 x 32

LEFT-
ARM
MODULE
32 x 32

OTTOMAN
22 x 22

OTTOMAN
20 x 27

OTTOMAN
16 x 30

OCCASIONAL
CHAIR
24 x 22

OCCASIONAL
CHAIR
25 x 20

OCCASIONAL
CHAIR
26 x 23

ARM-
CHAIR
27 x 27

ARM-
CHAIR
29 x 27

ROCKING
CHAIR
22 x 24

32"
ROUND
OTTOMAN

CHAISE LONGUE
24 x 60

KING SIZE
WITH HEADBOARD
80 x 83

MATTRESS
80 x 78

QUEEN SIZE
WITH HEADBOARD
80 x 64

MATTRESS
80 x 60

DOUBLE BED
WITH HEADBOARD
75 x 59

MATTRESS
75 x 54

TWIN BED
WITH
HEADBOARD
75 x 44

MATTRESS
75 x 39

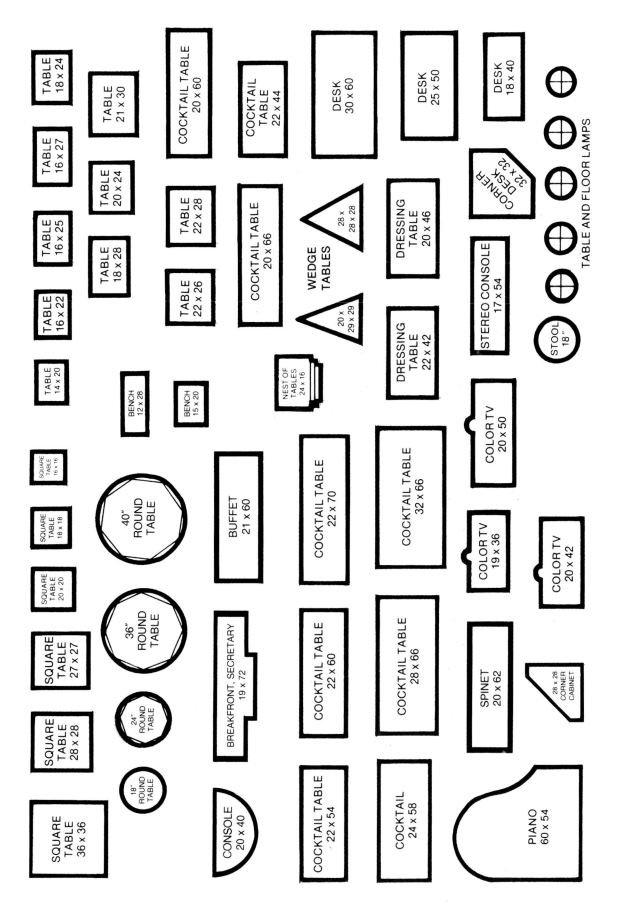

TABLE 18 x 24

TABLE 21 x 30

TABLE 16 x 27

TABLE 20 x 24

TABLE 16 x 25

TABLE 18 x 28

TABLE 16 x 22

TABLE 14 x 20

COCKTAIL TABLE 20 x 60

COCKTAIL TABLE 22 x 44

DESK 30 x 60

DESK 25 x 50

DESK 18 x 40

TABLE 22 x 28

TABLE 22 x 26

COCKTAIL TABLE 20 x 66

WEDGE TABLES

28 x 28 x 28

20 x 29 x 29

DRESSING TABLE 20 x 46

DRESSING TABLE 22 x 42

CORNER DESK 32 x 32

STEREO CONSOLE 17 x 54

STOOL 18"

TABLE AND FLOOR LAMPS

NEST OF TABLES 24 x 16

BENCH 12 x 28

BENCH 15 x 20

SQUARE TABLE 16 x 16

SQUARE TABLE 18 x 18

SQUARE TABLE 20 x 20

SQUARE TABLE 27 x 27

SQUARE TABLE 28 x 28

SQUARE TABLE 36 x 36

40" ROUND TABLE

36" ROUND TABLE

24" ROUND TABLE

18" ROUND TABLE

BUFFET 21 x 60

COCKTAIL TABLE 22 x 70

COCKTAIL TABLE 32 x 66

COLOR TV 20 x 50

COLOR TV 19 x 36

COLOR TV 20 x 42

BREAKFRONT, SECRETARY 19 x 72

COCKTAIL TABLE 22 x 60

COCKTAIL TABLE 28 x 66

SPINET 20 x 62

28 x 28 CORNER CABINET

CONSOLE 20 x 40

COCKTAIL TABLE 22 x 54

COCKTAIL 24 x 58

PIANO 60 x 54

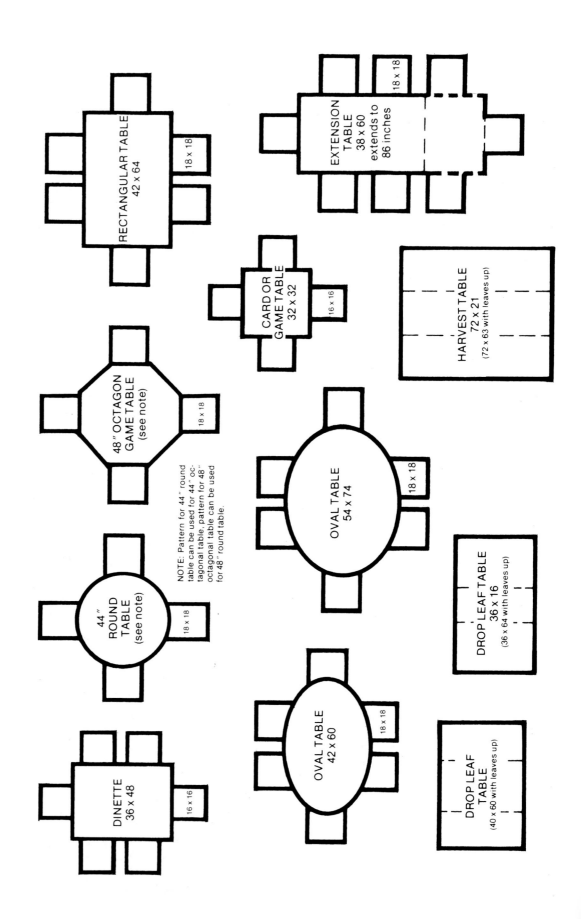

RECTANGULAR TABLE
42 x 64

18 x 18

EXTENSION
TABLE
38 x 60
extends to
86 inches

18 x 18

CARD OR
GAME TABLE
32 x 32

16 x 16

HARVEST TABLE
72 x 21
(72 x 63 with leaves up)

48" OCTAGON
GAME TABLE
(see note)

18 x 18

OVAL TABLE
54 x 74

18 x 18

NOTE: Pattern for 44" round
table can be used for 44" octagonal table, pattern for 48"
octagonal table can be used
for 48" round table.

44"
ROUND
TABLE
(see note)

18 x 18

DROP LEAF TABLE
36 x 16
(36 x 64 with leaves up)

DINETTE
36 x 48

16 x 16

OVAL TABLE
42 x 60

18 x 18

DROP LEAF
TABLE
(40 x 60 with leaves up)

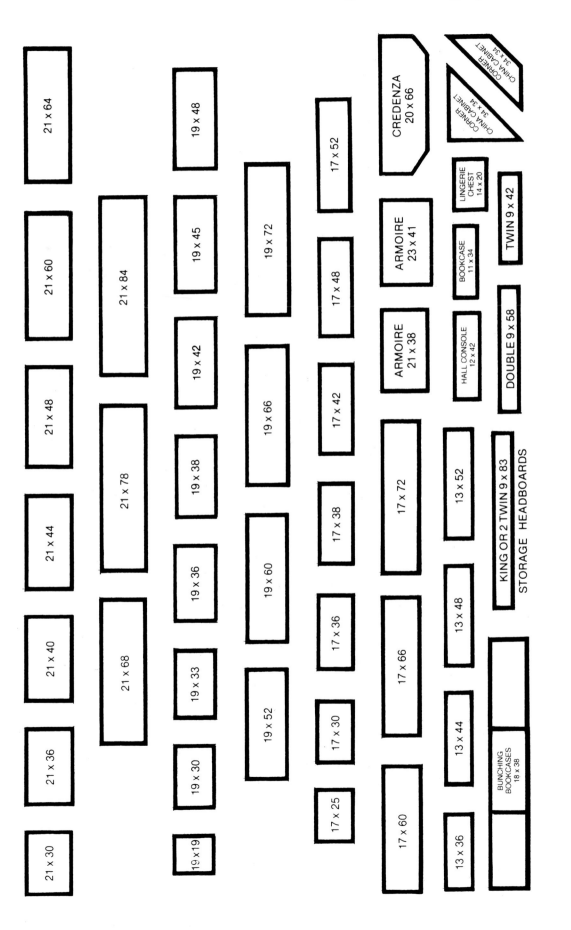

21 x 64

21 x 60

21 x 48

21 x 44

21 x 40

21 x 36

21 x 30

21 x 84

21 x 78

21 x 68

19 x 48

19 x 45

19 x 42

19 x 38

19 x 36

19 x 33

19 x 30

19 x 19

19 x 72

19 x 66

19 x 60

19 x 52

17 x 52

17 x 48

17 x 42

17 x 38

17 x 36

17 x 30

17 x 25

17 x 72

17 x 66

17 x 60

CREDENZA
20 x 66

ARMOIRE
23 x 41

ARMOIRE
21 x 38

CORNER
CHINA CABINET
34 x 34

CORNER
CHINA CABINET
34 x 34

LINGERIE
CHEST
14 x 20

BOOKCASE
11 x 34

HALL CONSOLE
12 x 42

TWIN 9 x 42

DOUBLE 9 x 58

13 x 52

13 x 48

13 x 44

13 x 36

KING OR 2 TWIN 9 x 83

STORAGE HEADBOARDS

BUNCHING
BOOKCASES
18 x 38

1 square=1 foot

index